THE BIG METRONOME

by
Bruce Arnold

Muse Eek Publishing Company
New York, New York

ISBN 1-890944-37-8

Printed in the United States

This publication can be purchased from your local bookstore or by contacting:
Muse Eek Publishing Company
550 Broadway 2nd Floor
New York, New York 10012
Phone: 212-226-9679   Fax 212-625-1839
website: www.muse-eek.com

Table Of Contents

Acknowledgments

The author would like to thank Michal Shapiro for her patience and help in proof reading and for her suggestions. I would also like to thank my students who through their questions allowed me to see their needs so that I might address them as best I could.

About the Author

Bruce Arnold is from Sioux Falls, South Dakota. His educational background started with 3 years of music study at the University of South Dakota; he then attended the Berklee College of Music where he received a Bachelor of Music degree in composition. During that time he also studied privately with Jerry Bergonzi and Charlie Banacos.

Mr. Arnold has taught at some of the most prestigious music schools in America, including the New England Conservatory of Music, Dartmouth College, Berklee College of Music, Princeton University and New York University. He is a performer, composer, jazz clinician and has an extensive private instruction practice.

Currently Mr. Arnold is performing with his own "The Bruce Arnold Trio," and "Eye Contact" with Harvie Swartz, as well as with two experimental bands, "Release the Hounds" a free improv group, and "Spooky Actions" which re-interprets the work of 20th Century classical masters.

His debut CD "Blue Eleven" (MMC 2036J) received great critical acclaim, and his newest CD "A Few Dozen" will be released in January 2000.

For more information about Mr. Arnold check his website at http://www.arnoldjazz.com This website contains audio examples of Mr. Arnold's compositions and a workshop section with free downloadable music exercises.

Foreword

Many of my students have asked me how they can improve their perception of time. This book is an attempt to fill those needs.

As your perception of time grows stronger so will your basic musicianship and creativity. You will also become a stronger ensemble player.

This book is part of a series dealing with time. Further information on the "time" series can be found at the back of this book.

Bruce Arnold
New York, New York

How to Use this book

The course of study presented in this book assumes that the reader has intermediate to advanced knowledge of music. With any course of study questions arise, therefore Muse-eek presents a forum where relevant questions will be answered by the author. Please visit the publisher's website at www.muse-eek.com first and check the FAQ section for this book to see if your question has already been answered. If not, use the form on the website to e-mail your questions.

This book is divided into 3 sections each corresponding to one of the enclosed CDs. Within each section different exercises will be presented to help develop your internal sense of time. You can work on a variety of different exercises at once or just concentrate on the areas you find the most challenging. Within each section the exercises are divided as follows:

1. Introduction
2. Technical Exercises
      A. Rhythm Techniques
      B. Melodic Techniques
      C. Harmonic Techniques
3. Creative Exercises
      A. Improvisation

First read through the "Introduction" to familiarize yourself with the basic theory. Depending on your ability you can then proceed to any section of the book you find intriguing. It is recommended that you work with some of the technical exercises first to gain some control. Many of the exercises presented in this book are excerpts from other books. If you find certain exercises particularly helpful, you may wish to do a larger study by working out of the excerpted book.

The methods presented in this book are only a few of the exercise possibilities. Be imaginative! Develop other exercises to use with the CDs. It can be as simple as reading through a piece of music, to practicing with a whole ensemble using the CDs.

Introduction

The Big Metronome is designed to help you develop a better internal sense of time. This is accomplished by requiring you to "feel time" rather than having you rely on the steady click of a metronome. The idea is to slowly wean yourself away from an external device and rely on your internal/natural sense of time. The exercises presented work in conjunction with the three CDs that accompany this book. CD 1 presents the first 13 settings from a traditional metronome 40-66; the second CD contains metronome markings 69-116, and the third CD contains metronome markings 120-208. The first CD gives you a 2 bar count off and a click every measure, the second CD gives you a 2 bar count off and a click every 2 measures, the 3rd CD gives you a 2 bar count off and a click every 4 measures. By presenting all common metronome markings a student can use these 3 CDs as a replacement for a traditional metronome.

Let's discuss the proper approach to this book and the idea of developing your own internal feel for time. This strong sense of time is not achieved by subdividing it in your head nor is it helped by tapping your foot or moving your body. It is achieved by trusting your internal clock based on a feeling rather than an intellectual or mechanical subdivision. Your goal is to just feel these larger groups of time, not to think about them. Humans have a remarkable built-in sense of time. If you give yourself the proper tools and the proper frame of mind you will find that through working with the CD and exercises presented in this book, you will be able to feel larger spaces of time. If you want to continue this process and work on feeling even larger spaces of time accurately, I recommend getting the Doing Time with the Blues ISBN #1890944173 and Doing Time with 32 Bars ISBN #189094422X

It should be mentioned at this point, that developing time *takes time*. Stopping your old process of counting time and beginning to just feel it is something that will develop over a period of weeks, not days. Stick with it, though, and you will start to really enjoy practicing with the CDs. For each exercise find a tempo that is comfortable for you to begin with and eventually try more challenging tempos. After you've worked with these CDs you will find it hard to go back to a regular metronome because it will seem overbearing and intrusive.

There are two approaches presented in this book; the technical and the creative. The technical way starts with developing your ability to play simple rhythms and other exercises with a pulse happening every two bars. You have to gain at least partial mastery of this before you can attempt to use the creative approach. The creative approach uses improvisation concepts to help you keep this internal time sense happening as you play and improvise. While the technical side may come more quickly than the creative approach, both compliment each other and help to build a strong internal time sense.

Introduction continued

Once you start feeling this larger sense of time you will have more ability to utilize time as you see fit. For instance if you are feeling time in 2 measure chunks you could subdivide that time up any way you want. On the technical side, you could play any number of beats you please during this two bar period. On the organic, creative side, you could experiment with tempo; speeding up part of the time and slowing down another part. This ability to mold time as you go is one of the exciting aspects of this way of feeling time. Obviously this has to be done in a musical way and in a musically appropriate place.

It is extremely difficult to give up counting and tapping one's foot to subdivide and keep time, but you want to start to *feel* time not *count* time. The exercises in this book will help you to do this.

Our first goal is to help you unlearn bad habits. It can't be stated enough: Believe that you as human have a good internal sense of time; you just need to develop it and rely on it more. Again it is important to gain a basic working ability with the technical side of this book before proceeding to the creative. With each exercise just try to sense the time moving in a larger period. Play the exercise until you hear it and are not relying on counting to play it correctly. Find a tempo and an exercise that is comfortable for you to start with; each person is different depending on ability.

As previously stated this book is divided into 3 overall sections. Use CD 1 to accompany the exercises found on the following pages.

Techniques

This section presents different ways of dividing up one bar time units using rhythm, melody and harmony. There is no end to the combinations you could explore using these three variables. Each set of exercises will explore some of the more common applications of this larger time sense. There is no particular sequence that you need to follow in this section, but it is recommended that you work on either the rhythmic or melodic techniques first, then proceed to the harmonic. After you gain a little control, try starting the creative exercises. Many of these exercises are excerpts from either previously published or forthcoming books. Their names and ISBN numbers have been provided with the exercises, or you can refer to the list of Muse Eek publications at the back of this book.

Rhythm Technique One

Rhythm Technique One will take you through 16 exercises that divide a one bar period of time into equal subdivisions. It is not necessary to master all these 16 exercises before proceeding to the next technique. Find a track on the CD that you feel comfortable with, and use that as a starting place. You will find that the more subdivisions of time you have in the exercise the easier it is to feel the time. You will also find that it is easier to 'feel' the time if you start with faster tempos. If you are having trouble with these exercises, try starting with track 8-10 which are faster. Remember to just feel and hear what this rhythm would sound like rather than counting it in your head.

Exercise 1: One beat for every bar

Exercise 2 Two beats for every bar

Exercise 3: Three beats for every bar. Note: you may find that starting with 6 beats per bar may help you before attempting 3 beats.

Exercise 4: Four beats for every bar

Exercise 5: Five beats for every bar

Exercise 6: Six beats for every bar

Exercise 7: Seven beats for every bar

Exercise 8: Eight beats for every bar

Exercise 9: Nine beats for every bar

Exercise 10: Ten beats for every bars

Exercise 11: Eleven beats for every bar

Exercise 12: Twelve beats for every bar

Exercise 13: Thirteen beats for every bar

Exercise 14: Fourteen beats for every bar

Exercise 15: Fifteen beats for every bar

Exercise 16: Sixteen beats for every bar

Rhythm Technique Two

Rhythm Technique Two will take you through 28 exercises which divide a one bar period of time into unequal subdivisions using eighth, sixteenth and thirty second notes. It is not necessary to master all these 28 exercises before proceeding to the next technique. Each track on the CD will make these exercises easier or harder depending on the tempo. Experiment to find which track is a good starting place for you. You can approach these exercises in two ways, for example: you can play all the eighth notes found in example one and accent the appropriate notes or play only the accented notes. You can also apply this unequal subdivision to all the exercises presented in Rhythm Technique One. This more advanced method will greatly strengthen your ability to subdivide a measure. But remember, always try to hear the rhythm rather than count it in your head. The following exercises are excerpts from "Accents Volume One" ISBN #1890944386

Exercise 1: A group of 3 and 5 within one bar

Exercise 2: A group of 5 and 3 within one bar

Exercise 3: Three groups divided 1-3-4 within one bar

Exercise 4: Three groups divided 1-4-3 within one bar

Exercise 5: Three groups divided 3-1-4 within one bar

Exercise 6: Three groups divided 3-4-1 within one bar

Exercise 7: Three groups divided 4-1-3 within one bar

Exercise 8: Three groups divided 4-3-1 within one bar

Exercise 9: Three groups divided 1-2-5 within one bar

Exercise 10: Three groups divided 1-5-2 within one bar

Exercise 11: Three groups divided 2-1-5 within one bar

Exercise 12: Three groups divided 2-5-1 within one bar

Exercise 13: Three groups divided 5-1-2 within one bar

Exercise 14: Two groups divided 7-9 within one bar

Exercise 15: Two groups divided 9-7 within one bar

Exercise 16: Three groups divided 5-4-7 within one bar

Exercise 17: Three groups divided 7-4-5 within one bar

Exercise 18: Four groups divided 3-4-6-3 within one bar

Exercise 19: Three groups divided 6-7-3 within one bar

Exercise 20: Three groups divided 7-6-3 within one bar

Exercise 21: Four groups divided 3-3-5-5 within one bar

Exercise 22: Four groups divided 5-5-3-3 within one bar

Exercise 23: Four groups divided 5-4-4-3 within one bar

Exercise 24: Four groups divided 9-9-9-7 within one bar

Exercise 25: Six groups divided 5-5-5-5-7 within one bar

Exercise 26: Five groups divided 7-7-7-7-5 within one bar

Exercise 27: Seven groups divided 5-5-4-5-4-5-5 within one bar

Exercise 28: Ten groups divided 3-3-3-3-3-3-3-4-4-3 within one bar

Rhythm Technique Three

Rhythm Technique Three will take you through 8 exercises which present various rhythm patterns in a one bar period of time. It is not necessary to master all these 8 exercises before proceeding to the next technique. Each track on the CD will make these exercises easier or harder depending on the tempo. Experiment to find which track is a good starting place for you. The following exercises are excerpts from "Rhythms Volume One" ISBN #0964863278

Exercise 1

Exercise 2

Exercise 3

Exercise 4

Rhythm Technique Four

Rhythm Technique Four will take you through 4 exercises which present various rhythm patterns in a one bar period of time. It is not necessary to master all these 8 exercises before proceeding to the next technique. Each track on the CD will make these exercises easier or harder depending on the tempo. Experiment to find which track is a good starting place for you. The following exercises are excerpts from "Rhythms Volume Two" ISBN #0964863286

Exercise 1

Exercise 2

Exercise 3

Exercise 4

Rhythm Technique Five

Rhythm Technique Five will take you through 9 exercises which present various rhythm patterns in a one bar period of time. It is not necessary to master all these 9 exercises before proceeding to the next technique. Each track on the CD will make these exercises easier or harder depending on the tempo. Experiment to find which track is a good starting place for you. The following exercises are excerpts from "Rhythm Primer" ISBN #1890944033 and "Rhythms Volume Three" ISBN #0964863286

Exercise 1

Exercise 2

Exercise 3

Exercise 4

Exercise 5

Exercise 6

Exercise 7

Exercise 8

Exercise 9

Rhythm Technique Six

Rhythm Technique Six will take you through 25 exercises that promote a strong sense of time through development of independence within a two measure grouping. Play each part using a different limb. Work through all combinations to get the most out of this technique. The following is a list of possible combinations:

Right Hand	Left Hand
Right Hand	Right Foot
Right Hand	Left Foot
Left Hand	Right Hand
Left Hand	Left Foot
Left Hand	Right Foot
Right Foot	Left Foot
Right Foot	Right Hand
Right Foot	Left Hand
Left Foot	Right Foot
Left Foot	Left Hand
Left Foot	Right Hand

It is not necessary to <u>master</u> all these 25 exercises before proceeding to the next technique. Each track on the CD will make these exercises easier or harder depending on the tempo. Experiment to find which tempo is a good starting place for you. Some of the following are excerpts from Independence Volume One ISBN # 1890944009.

Exercise 1:

Exercise 2:

Exercise 3

Exercise 4

Exercise 5

Exercise 6

Exercise 7

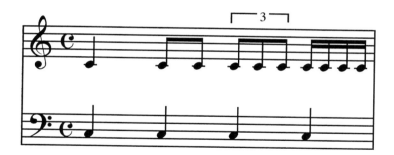

Exercise 8

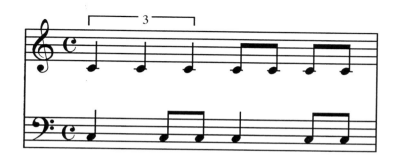

Exercise 9

Exercise 10

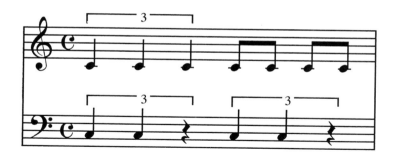

Exercise 11

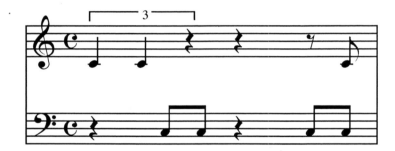

Exercise 12

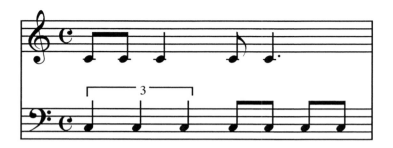

Exercise 13

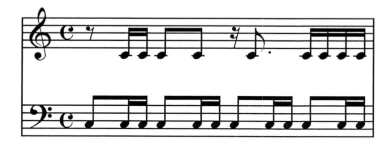

Exercise 14

Exercise 15

Exercise 16

Exercise 17

Exercise 18

Exercise 19

Exercise 20

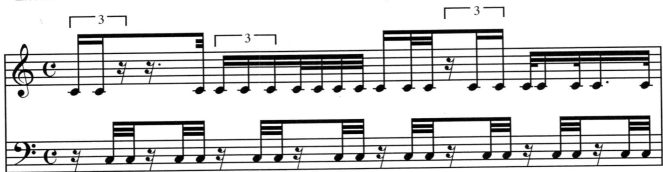

Exercise 21

Exercise 22

Exercise 23

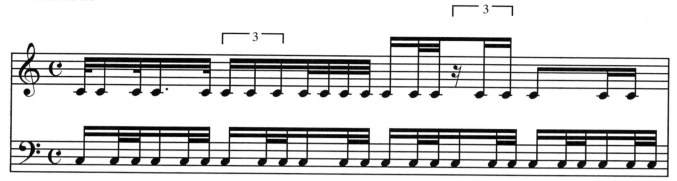

Exercise 24

Exercise 25

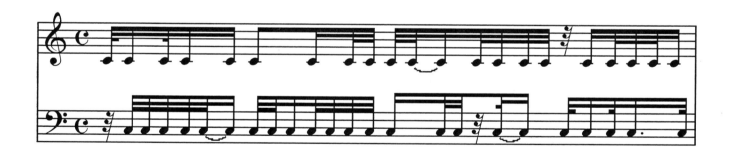

Melodic Techniques

Melodic Techniques to develop control within a one measure grouping can be approached many ways. The following exercises will show some of the ways you can develop a longer rhythmic sense and how this longer rhythmic sense can affect your melodic choices. You will find that thinking in a longer basic rhythm can have profound impact on your phrasing, rhythmic choices and melodic direction. The following exercises explore some of those choices.

Melodic Technique One

Melodic Technique One shows 2 exercises which show some of the possible ways a one measure grouping can effect the rhythmic placement of a melodic line. Example 1 and 2 present an example of a scale that can be used to create a melodic pattern that will repeat every one bar. Example 1 is a simple pentatonic scale which when played in eighth notes in a sixteen note grouping will always repeat itself every bar. Example 2 shows a major scale which when sequenced in eighth notes in a 24 note pattern will repeat itself every bar. Pick various scales and melodic patterns that repeat every two bars and you can reinforce your feeling of a one bar phrase. Experiment with the rhythmic patterns found in the Rhythm Technique One section and you will find many new ways of playing melodically over one bar.

Exercise 1 is an example of playing a pentatonic scale in a regular phrasing pattern.

Exercise 2 is an example of playing a major scale in a regular phrasing pattern.

Melodic Technique Two

   Melodic Technique Two will take you through 7 exercises which show how an irregular phrasing pattern can help to create variation within a melodic pattern. Example 1 shows an 16 note pattern in constant eighth notes. This creates an irregular pattern that only repeats itself every two bars. Example 2 shows an 8 note pattern in constant eighth notes triplets. This creates an irregular pattern that only repeats itself every two bars. Pick various scales and melodic patterns that repeat every two bars and you can reinforce your feeling for a two bar phrase. Experiment with the rhythmic patterns found in Rhythm Technique One and you will find many new ways of playing by superimposing different phrasing combinations.

Exercise 1

Exercise 2

Exercise 3 presents a 6 note scale that has irregular phrasing. This melodic pattern repeats itself every 10 notes but it takes 5 measures before the pattern is back to starting on 'one'. You will notice by looking at the markers that you start on a different note every measure. By practicing with larger melodic passages you will become aware of how your phrasing of these exercises changes, as opposed to using a metronome, where you don't have the feeling of a group, but only a constant click that doesn't define the downbeat of the measure.

Exercise 3

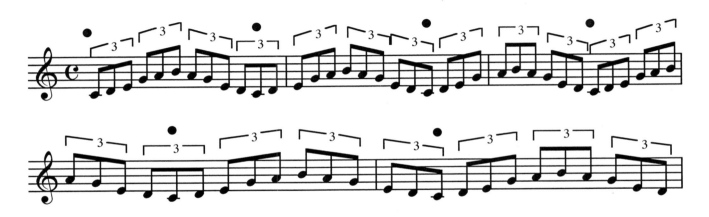

Exercise 4 presents a 10 note arpeggio which has irregular phrasing. This melodic pattern repeats itself every 10 notes but it takes 5 measures before the pattern is back to starting on 'one'.

Exercise 4

Exercise 5 presents a 4 note arpeggio which has irregular phrasing. This melodic pattern repeats itself every 8 notes but it takes 4 measures before the pattern is back to starting on 'one'.

Exercise 5

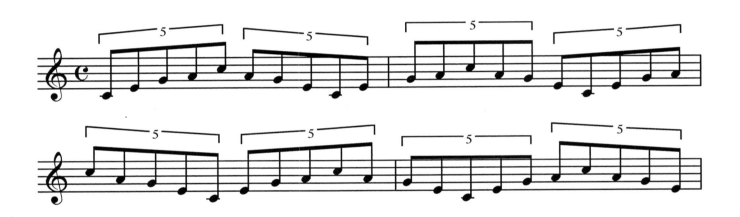

Exercise 6 presents a 4 note scale which has irregular phrasing. This melodic pattern repeats itself every 6 notes but it takes 6 measures before the pattern is back to starting on 'one'.

Exercise 6

Exercise 7 presents a 2 note scale which has irregular phrasing. This melodic pattern repeats itself every 7 notes but it takes 7 measures before the pattern is back to starting on 'one'.

Exercise 7

Melodic Technique Three

Melodic Technique Three involves playing melodies or heads to work on your ability to play an entire melody with just one click every bar. You could use any head found in a fake book. On the next page I have given you a composition of mine. Try playing this with various tracks on the CD. I originally wrote it to be played at quarter note equals 120, but try other metronome markings as well.

MacDougal St.

SWING
INTRO

Composer Bruce Arnold

To A for solos
Solo Form AAB

Harmonic Techniques

Traditional harmonic techniques for a one bar period of time are limited unless the tempo is slow. To develop a feel for playing chords with a click every measure, play along with the chord progression found in the Harmonic Techniques for CD 2 and 3.

One area that could use some exploration is playing/writing more contrapuntally within a one bar phrase. Technique One will explore a composition I wrote entitled "Dialog" By using one measure segments of this excerpt you can explore different harmonic movement within a measure. Try writing your own contrapuntal exercises to explore this in more depth. Dialog can be heard on The Bruce Arnold Trio CD entitled "A Few Dozen"

DIALOG

Composer Bruce Arnold

Guitar to D tuning

Creative Technique

I have written repeatedly about the creative approach, yet there is very little that one can do to teach this particular aspect of music. This is something that comes from within, and the best that any teacher can do is to provide every possible tool for the student so that there is no impediment to the creative process. Presenting more techniques of improvisation just brings us back to a technical side of music. It is best that you use this section of the book as a springboard for your self expression.

I have included some solo forms using the traditional major and minor blues. As with all solo forms there are infinite variations you can use to practice and be creative. Much of your direction in this section depends on your instrument. If you are a drummer or a piano player your can just play time or play the chords. If you are a saxophonist you may express yourself in a multitude of ways, from free form blowing to structured scales. It all depends on where you are with music and where you are going. This is why for this section of the book I have just supplied some chord progressions that you can use to improvise with. Experiment and try different approaches to test your ability to keep time flowing correctly. From the work you have done in the technical section of this book you should find that you are able to function more efficiently within a one bar phrase. The real challenge comes when you let go and completely trust your internal clock as you improvise. This is the key to letting your inner voice speak. It is a lifelong pursuit for the artist that is within you.

12 Bar Blues in Gb

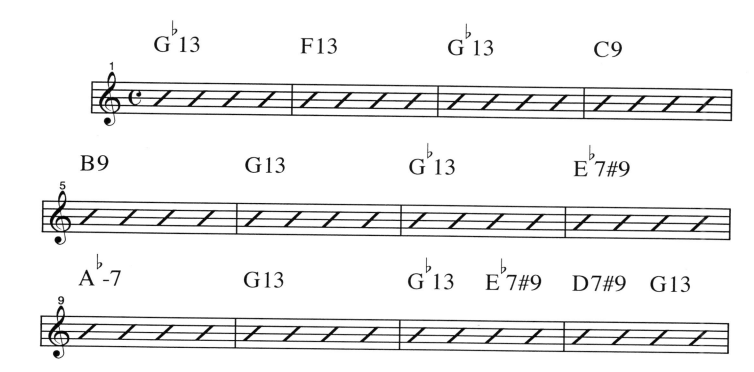

12 Bar Blues in B

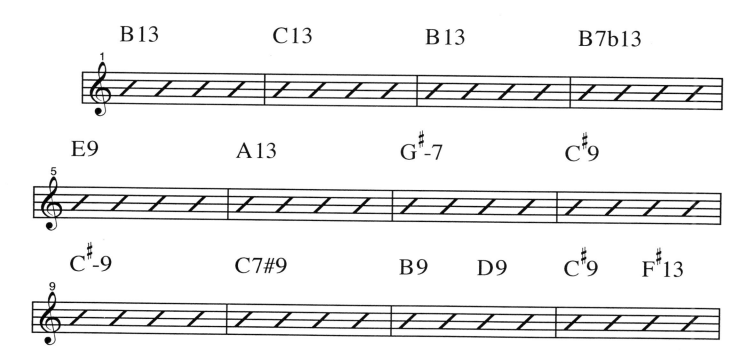

Ab Minor Blues

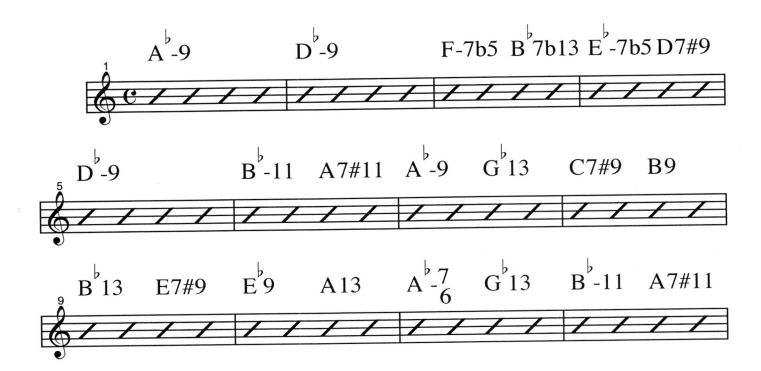

Db Minor Blues

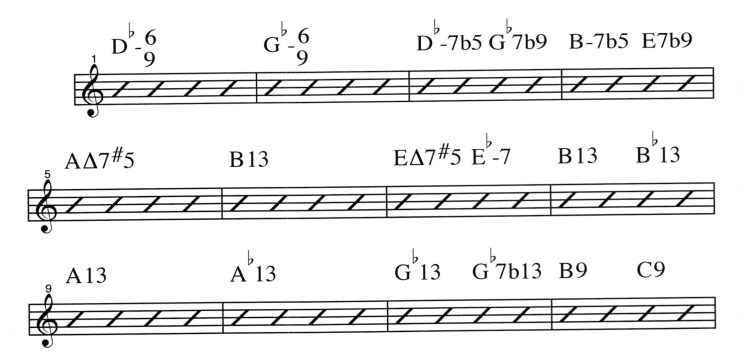

Gb Minor Blues

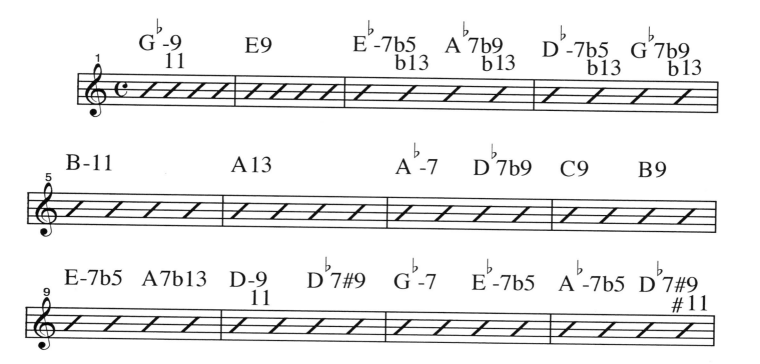

B Minor Blues

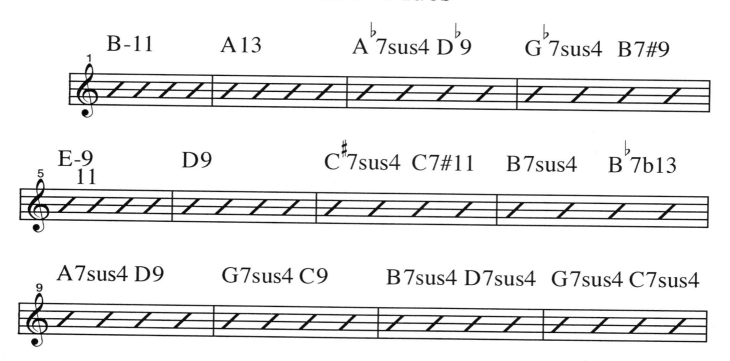

D Minor Blues

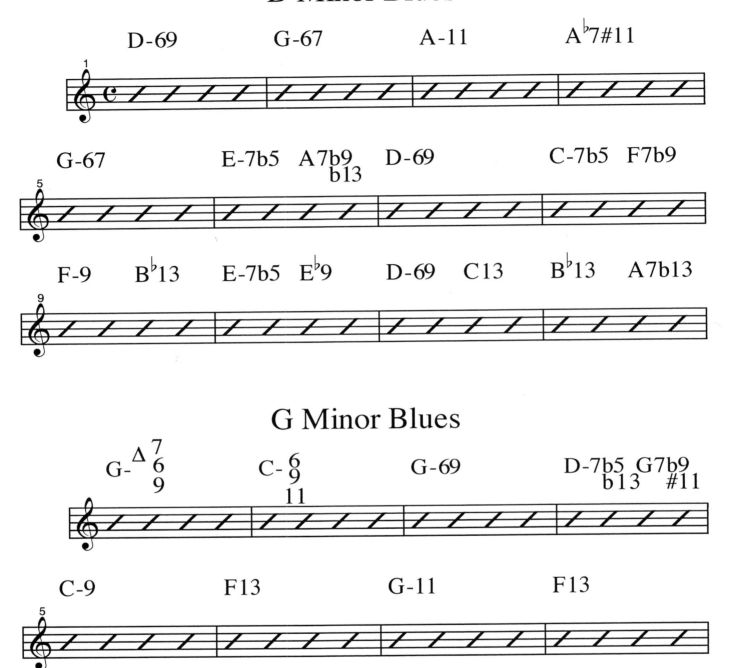

G Minor Blues

Techniques for CD 2

CD 2

This second section will present you with many pages of exercises to develop your sense of a two bar interval on time. Many of the exercises, especially the chord progressions, can also be applied to CD 1 and 3.

Techniques

This section presents different ways of dividing up these larger 2 bar time units using rhythm, melody and harmony. There is no end to the combinations you could explore using these three variables. Each set of exercises will explore some of the more common applications of this larger time sense. There is no particular sequence that you need to maintain in this techniques section. It is recommended that you work on either the rhythmic or melodic techniques first then proceed to the harmonic. When you gain a little control try starting the creative exercises. Many of these exercises are excerpts from either previously published or forthcoming books. Their names and ISBN numbers have been provided with the exercises, or you can refer to the list of Muse Eek publications at the back of this book.

Rhythm Technique One

Rhythm Technique One will take you through 16 exercises that divide a two bar period of time into equal subdivisions. It is not necessary to master all these 16 exercises before proceeding to the next technique. Find a track on the CD that you feel comfortable with and use that as a starting place. You will find that the more subdivisions of time you have in the exercise the easier it is to feel the time. For example: exercise eight played with track 8-10 is a good place to start if you are having difficulties. Remember to try to just feel and hear what this rhythm would sound like rather than counting it in your head

Exercise 1: One beat for every two bars

Exercise 2 Two beats for every two bars

Exercise 3: Three beats for every two bars. Note: you may find that starting with 6 beats per bar may help you before attempting 3 beats.

Exercise 4: Four beats for every two bars

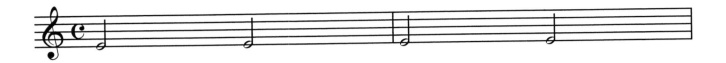

Exercise 5: Five beats for every two bars

Exercise 6: Six beats for every two bars

Exercise 7: Seven beats for every two bars

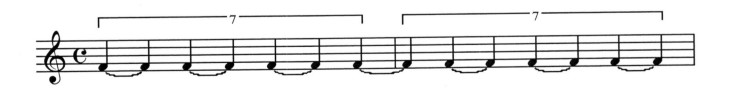

Exercise 6: Eight beats for every two bars

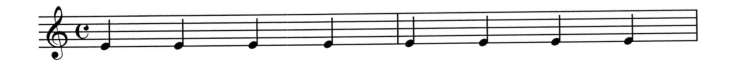

Exercise 9: Nine beats for every two bars

Exercise 10: Ten beats for every two bars

Exercise 11: Eleven beats for every two bars

Exercise 12: Twelve beats for every two bars

Exercise 13: Thirteen beats for every two bars

Exercise 14: Fourteen beats for every two bars

Exercise 15: Fifteen beats for every two bars

Exercise 16: Sixteen beats for every two bars

Rhythm Technique Two

Rhythm Technique Two will take you through 28 exercises which divide a two bar period of time into unequal subdivisions. It is not necessary to master all these 28 exercises before proceeding to the next technique. Each track on the CD will make these exercises easier or harder depending on their tempo. Experiment to find which track is a good starting place for you. You can approach these exercises in two ways: play all the quarter notes and accent the appropriate notes or play only the accented notes. You can also apply this unequal subdivision to all the exercises presented in Rhythm Technique One. This more advanced approach will greatly strengthen your ability to subdivide 2 measures. But remember, always try to hear the rhythm rather than count it in your head. The following exercises are excerpts from "Accents Volume One" ISBN #1890944386

Exercise 1: A group of 3 and 5 within two bars

Exercise 2: A group of 5 and 3 within two bars

Exercise 3: Three groups divided 1-3-4 within two bars

Exercise 4: Three groups divided 1-4-3 within two bars

Exercise 5: Three groups divided 3-1-4 within two bars

Exercise 6: Three groups divided 3-4-1 within two bars

Exercise 7: Three groups divided 4-1-3 within two bars

Exercise 8: Three groups divided 4-3-1 within two bars

Exercise 9: Three groups divided 1-2-5 within two bars

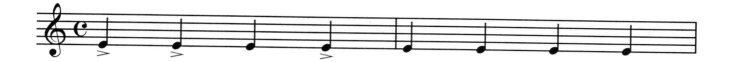

Exercise 10: Three groups divided 1-5-2 within two bars

Exercise 11: Three groups divided 2-1-5 within two bars

Exercise 12: Three groups divided 2-5-1 within two bars

Exercise 13: Three groups divided 5-1-2 within two bars

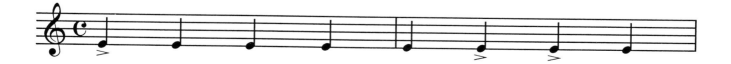

Exercise 14: Three groups divided 5-2-1 within two bars

Exercise 15: Three groups divided 2-3-3 within two bars

Exercise 16: Three groups divided 3-2-3 within two bars

Exercise 17: Three groups divided 3-3-2 within two bars

Exercise 18: Four groups divided 1-2-2-3 within two bars

Exercise 19: Four groups divided 1-2-3-2 within two bars

Exercise 20: Four groups divided 1-3-2-2 within two bars

Exercise 21: Four groups divided 2-1-2-3 within two bars

Exercise 22: Four groups divided 2-1-3-2 within two bars

Exercise 23: Four groups divided 2-2-1-3 within two bars

Exercise 24: Four groups divided 2-2-3-1 within two bars

Exercise 25: Four groups divided 2-3-2-1 within two bars

Exercise 26: Four groups divided 3-1-2-2 within two bars

Exercise 27: Four groups divided 3-2-1-2 within two bars

Exercise 28: Four groups divided 3-2-2-1 within two bars

Rhythm Technique Three

Rhythm Technique Three will take you through 8 exercises which present various rhythm patterns in a two bar period of time. It is not necessary to master all these 8 exercises before proceeding to the next technique. Each track on the CD will make these exercises easier or harder depending on the tempo. Experiment to find which track is a good starting place for you. The following exercises are excerpts from "Rhythms Volume One" ISBN #0964863278

Exercise 1

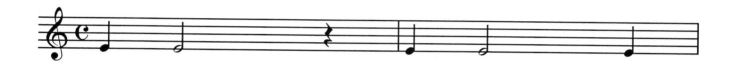

Exercise 2

Exercise 3

Exercise 4

Exercise 5

Exercise 6

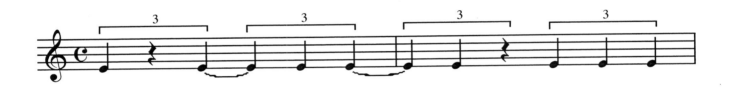

Exercise 7

Exercise 8

Rhythm Technique Four

Rhythm Technique Four will take you through 8 sixteenth note exercises which present various rhythm patterns in a two bar period of time. It is not necessary to master all these 8 exercises before proceeding to the next technique. Each track on the CD will make these exercises easier or harder depending on the tempo. Experiment to find which track is a good starting place for you. The following exercises are excerpts from "Rhythms Volume Two" ISBN #0964863286

Exercise 1

Exercise 2

Exercise 3

Exercise 4

Exercise 5

Exercise 6

Exercise 7

Exercise 8

Rhythm Technique Five

Rhythm Technique Five will take you through 8 exercises which present various odd meter combinations within a two bar period of time. First work on feeling the overall rhythm by playing only on 'one' of each measure. Then attempt the written rhythm. It is not necessary to master all these 8 exercises before proceeding to the next technique. Each track on the CD will make these exercises easier or harder depending on the tempo. Experiment to find which track is a good starting place for you. The following exercises are excerpts from "Odd Meters" ISBN #0964863294

Exercise 1

Exercise 2

Exercise 3

Exercise 4

Exercise 5

Exercise 6

Exercise 7

Exercise 8

Rhythm Technique Six

Rhythm Technique Six will take you through 25 exercises which promote a strong sense of time through development of independence within a two measure grouping. Play each part using a different limb. Work through all combinations to fully develop this technique. The following is a list of possible combinations:

Right Hand	Left Hand
Right Hand	Right Foot
Right Hand	Left Foot
Left Hand	Right Hand
Left Hand	Left Foot
Left Hand	Right Foot
Right Foot	Left Foot
Right Foot	Right Hand
Right Foot	Left Hand
Left Foot	Right Foot
Left Foot	Left Hand
Left Foot	Right Hand

It is not necessary to master all these 25 exercises before proceeding to the next technique. Each track on the CD will make these exercises easier or harder depending on the tempo. Experiment to find which tempo is a good starting place for you. The following are excerpts from Independence Volume One ISBN # 1890944009.

Exercise 1:

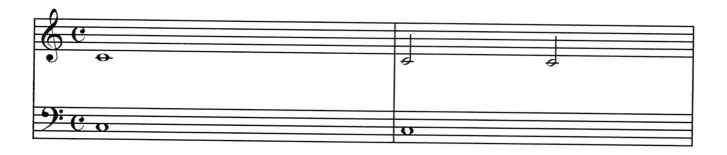

Exercise 2:

Exercise 3

Exercise 4

Exercise 5

Exercise 6

Exercise 7

Exercise 8

Exercise 9

Exercise 10

Exercise 11

Exercise 12

Exercise 13

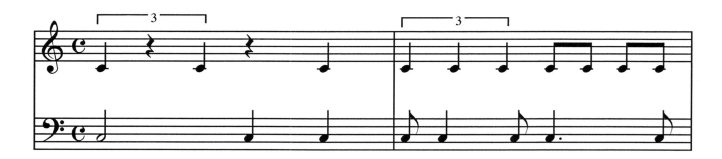

Exercise 14

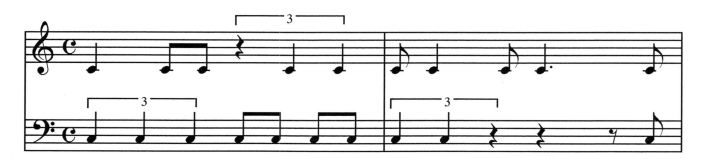

Exercise 15

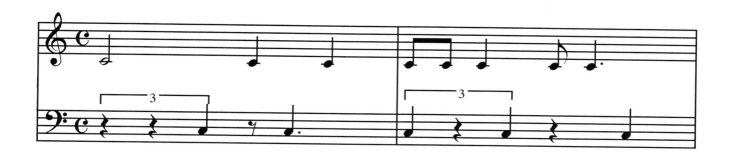

Exercise 16

Exercise 17

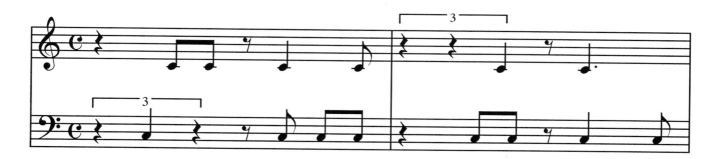

Exercise 18

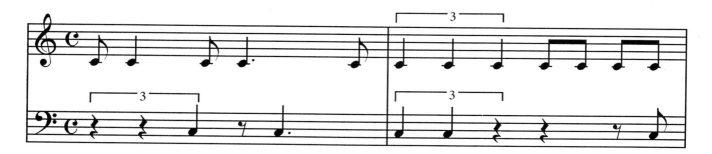

Exercise 19

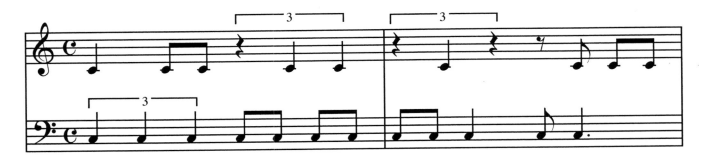

Exercise 20

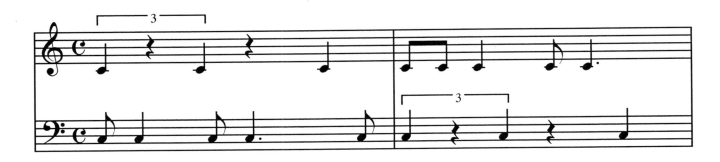

Exercise 21

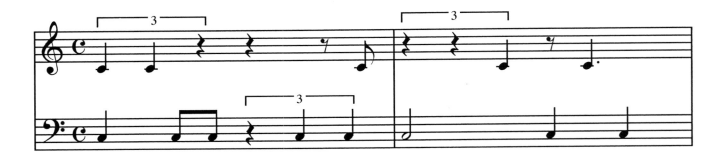

Exercise 22

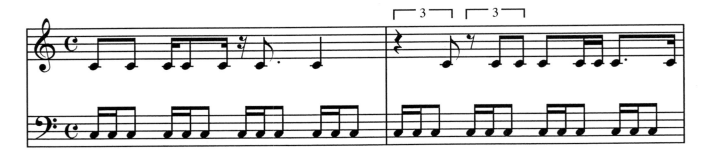

Exercise 23

Exercise 24

Exercise 25

Melodic Techniques

Melodic Techniques to develop control within a two measure grouping can be approached many ways. The following example will show some of the ways you can develop a longer rhythmic sense and how this longer rhythmic sense can affect your melodic choices. You will find that thinking in a longer basic rhythm can have profound impact on your phrasing, rhythmic choices and melodic direction. The following exercises explore some of those choices.

Melodic Technique One

Melodic Technique One shows 2 exercises which show some of the possible ways a two measure grouping can effect the rhythmic placement of a melodic line. Example 1 and 2 present an example of a scale that can be used to create a melodic pattern that will repeat every two bars. Example 1 is a simple pentatonic scale which when played in eighth notes in a sixteen note grouping will always repeat itself every two bars. Example 2 shows a major scale which when sequenced in eighth notes in a 24 note pattern will repeat itself every two bars. Pick various scales and melodic patterns that repeat every two bars and you can reinforce your feeling of a two bar phrase. Experiment with the rhythmic patterns found in the Rhythm Technique One section and you will find many new ways of playing melodically over two bars.

Exercise 1 is an example of playing a pentatonic scale in a regular phrasing pattern.

Exercise 2 is an example of playing a major scale in a regular phrasing pattern.

Melodic Technique Two

Melodic Technique Two will take you through 7 exercises which show how an irregular phrasing pattern can help to create variation within a melodic pattern. Example 1 shows an 18 note pattern in constant eighth notes. This creates an irregular pattern that only repeats itself every 14 bars. You will notice by looking at the markers every two bars that you start on a different note every two measures. By practicing with a two bar increment you become aware of how your phrasing of these exercises changes, as opposed to using a metronome, where you don't have the feeling of a group, but only a constant click that doesn't define the downbeat. Pick various scales and melodic patterns that repeat every two bars and you can reinforce your feeling for a two bar phrase. Experiment with the rhythmic patterns found in Rhythm Technique One and you will find many new ways of playing melodically over two bars.

Exercise 1

Exercise 2 presents a 7 note scale which has irregular phrasing. This melodic pattern repeats itself every 15 notes but it takes 15 measures before the pattern is back to starting on 'one'.

Exercise 2

Exercise 3 presents a 5 note minor pentatonic scale which has irregular phrasing. This melodic pattern repeats itself every 23 notes but it takes 12 measures before the pattern is back to starting on 'one'.

Exercise 3

Exercise 4 presents a 4 note scale which has irregular phrasing. This melodic pattern repeats itself every 19 notes but it takes 10 measures before the pattern is back to starting on 'one'.

Exercise 4

Exercise 5 presents a 3 note scale which has irregular phrasing. This melodic pattern repeats itself every 7 notes but it takes 7 measures before the pattern is back to starting on 'one'.

Exercise 5

Exercise 6 presents a 2 note scale which has irregular phrasing. This melodic pattern repeats itself every 7 notes but it takes 7 measures before the pattern is back to starting on 'one'.

Exercise 6

Melodic Technique Three

Melodic Technique Three involves playing Blues melodies, or "heads," to improve your ability to play an entire 12 bar melody with just one click every two bars. You could use any head found in a fake book. Some common examples of Jazz 12 bar blues are:

Au Privave
Blue Monk
Blues for Alice
Blue Train

On the next page I have given you a rather challenging head to a 12 Bar Blues entitled "A Few Dozen". Try playing this with various tracks on the CD. If you would like to hear a recording of this check out The Bruce Arnold Trio, "A Few Dozen" release date 1/1/2000.

A Few Dozen

Composer Bruce Arnold

♩=200
Swing

A Few Dozen Bass Part

Composer Bruce Arnold

♩=200
Swing

Harmonic Techniques

Harmonic Techniques to develop control within a two measure grouping can be approached many ways. I will mention a few here to get you started. One of the most exciting applications of this two bar period of time is to combine the previously discussed rhythm techniques with chord progressions. Also you can try some of the more obvious applications of the two bar grouping over 12 bar blues forms.

Harmonic Technique One

Harmonic Technique One presents 3 exercises where a harmonic framework is superimposed over some of the 2 measure rhythmic groupings presented on pages 3-6. It is beyond the scope of this book to explain the theories behind these chord progressions. A partial explanation of some of these techniques can be found in Chord Workbook for Guitar Volume One and Two
ISBN # 0964863219 and 0964863235.

Exercise 1: Use over 1st two bars of 12 Bar Blues in C

Exercise 2: Use over bars 3 and 4 of a 12 Bar Blues in C

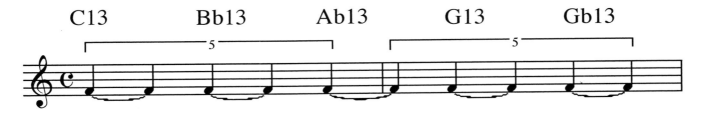

Exercise 3: Use over last two bars of a 12 Bar Blues in C

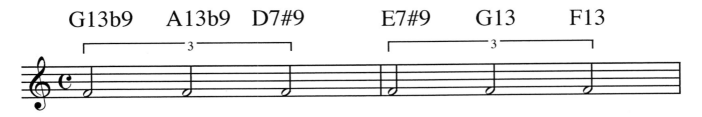

Harmonic Technique Two

Harmonic Technique Two presents two 12 bar chord progressions that can be used to develop an ability to play chords through a blues progression. If you play a melodic instrument try playing the chords as arpeggios. If you would like more 12 bar blues progressions I recommend Chord Workbook for Guitar Volume One ISBN # 0964863219 which contains 24 twelve bar blues progressions.

12 Bar Blues in C

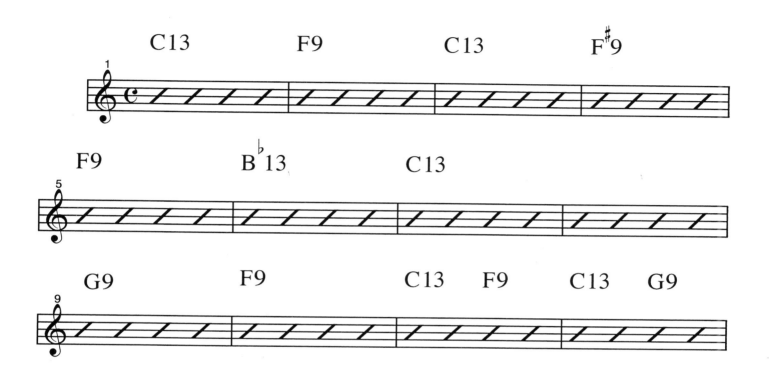

12 Bar Blues in F

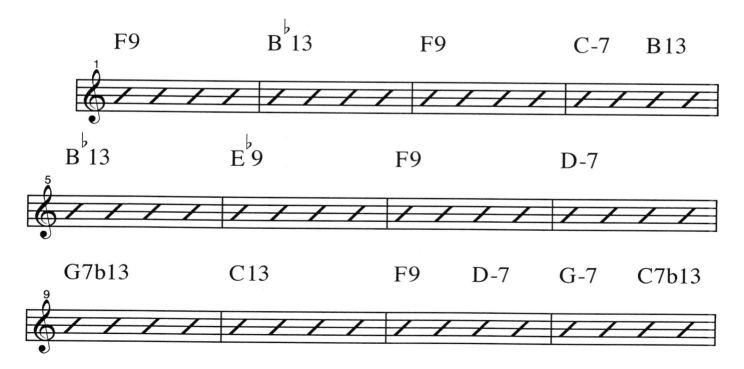

Creative Technique

I have written repeatedly about the creative approach, yet there is very little that one can do to teach this particular aspect of music. This is something that comes from within, and the best that any teacher can do is to provide every possible tool for the student so that there is no impediment to the creative process. Presenting more techniques of improvisation just brings us back to a technical side of music. It is best that you use this section of the book as a springboard for your self expression.

I have included some solo forms using the traditional major and minor blues. As with all solo forms there are infinite variations you can use to practice and be creative. Much of your direction in this section depends on your instrument. If you are a drummer or a piano player your can just play time or play the chords. If you are a saxophonist you may express yourself in a multitude of ways, from free form blowing to structured scales. It all depends on where you are with music and where you are going. This is why for this section of the book I have just supplied some chord progressions that you can use to improvise with. Experiment and try different approaches to test your ability to keep time flowing correctly. From the work you have done in the technical section of this book you should find that you are able to function more efficiently within a 2 bar phrase. The real challenge comes when you let go and completely trust your internal clock as you improvise. This is the key to letting your inner voice speak. It is a lifelong pursuit for the artist that is within you.

12 Bar Blues in Bb

12 Bar Blues in Eb

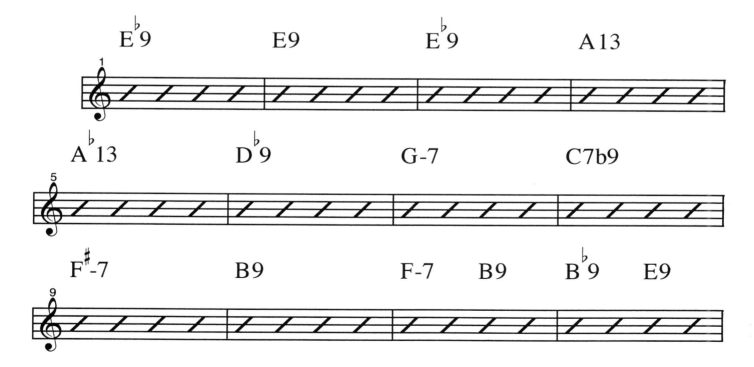

12 Bar Blues in Ab

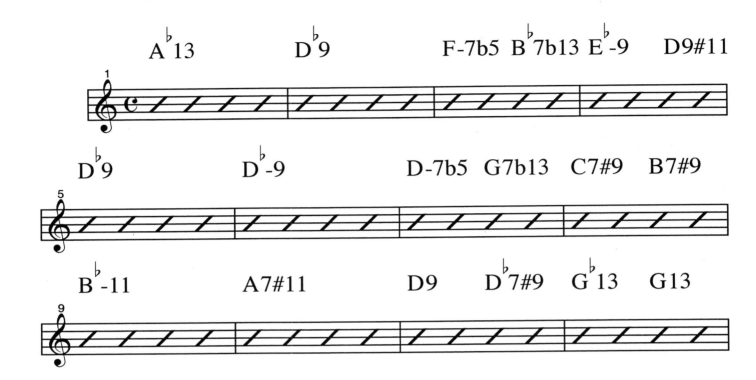

12 Bar Blues in Db

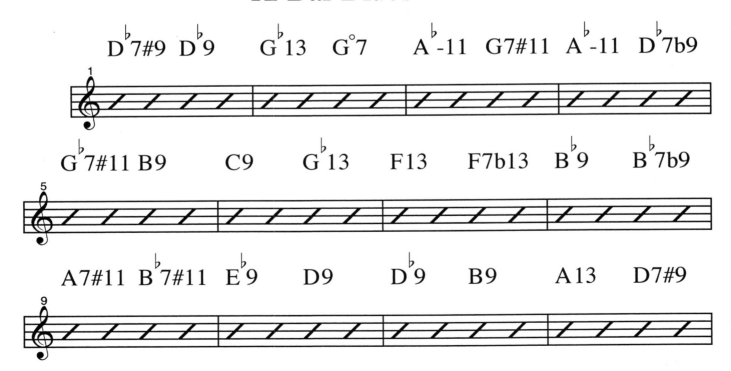

C Minor Blues

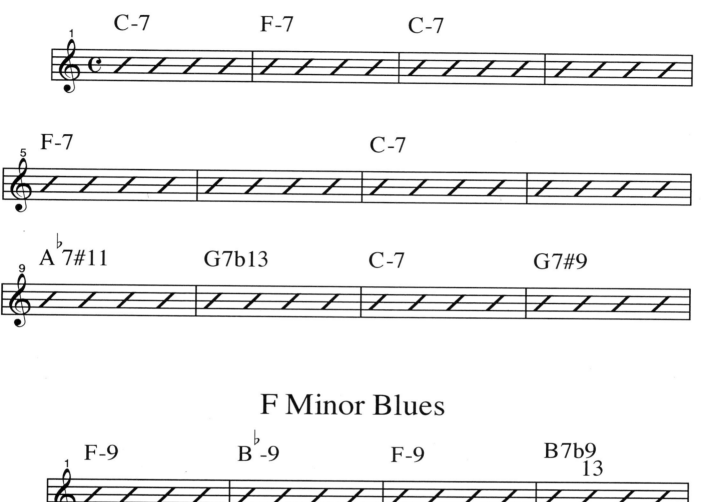

F Minor Blues

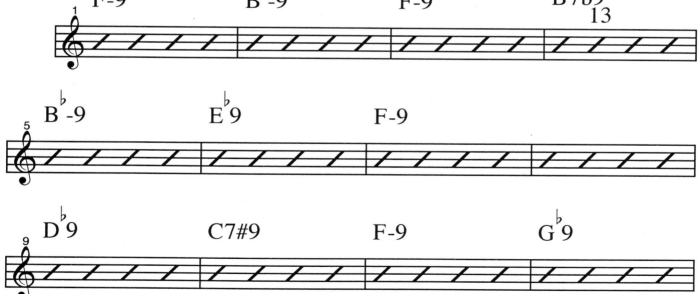

Bb Minor Blues

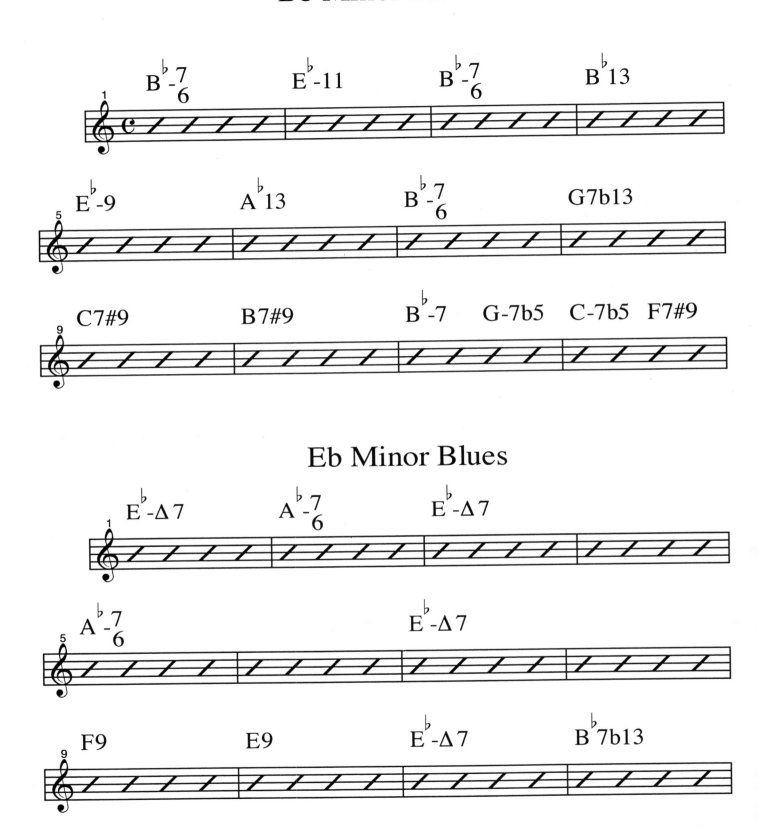

Eb Minor Blues

Techniques for CD 3

CD 3

This third section will present you with many pages of exercises to develop your sense of a four bar interval on time. Many of the exercises, especially the chord progressions, can also be applied to CD 1 and 2.

Techniques

This section presents different ways of dividing up these larger 4 bar time units using rhythm, melody and harmony. There is no end to the combinations you could explore using these three variables. Each set of exercises will explore some of the more common applications of this larger time sense. There is no particular sequence that you need to follow in this techniques section, but it is recommended that you work on either the rhythmic or melodic techniques first then proceed to the harmonic. After you gain a little control try starting the creative exercises. Many of these exercises are excerpts from either previously published or forthcoming books. Their names and ISBN numbers have been provided with the exercises, or you can refer to the list of Muse Eek publications at the back of this book.

Rhythm Technique One

Rhythm Technique One will take you through 16 exercises that divide a four bar period of time into equal subdivisions. It is not necessary to master all these 16 exercises before proceeding to the next technique. Find a track on the CD that you feel comfortable with, and use that as a starting place. You will find that the more subdivisions of time you have in the exercise the easier it is to feel the time. For example: exercise eight played with track 1-3 is a good place to start if you are having difficulties. Remember to try to just feel and hear what this rhythm would sound like rather than counting it in your head

Exercise 1: One beat for every four bars

Exercise 2 Two beats for every four bars

Exercise 3: Three beats for every four bars. Note: you may find that starting with 6 beats per bar may help you before attempting 3 beats.

Exercise 4: Four beats for every four bars

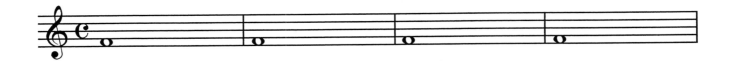

Exercise 5: Five beats for every four bars

Exercise 6: Six beats for every four bars

Exercise 7: Seven beats for every four bars

Exercise 8: Eight beats for every four bars

Exercise 9: Nine beats for every four bars

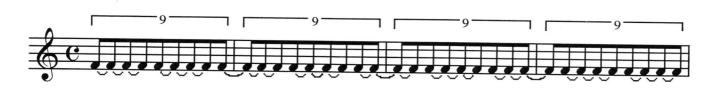

Exercise 10: Ten beats for every four bars

Exercise 11: Eleven beats for every four bars

Exercise 12: Twelve beats for every four bars

Exercise 13: Thirteen beats for every four bars

Exercise 14: Fourteen beats for every four bars

Exercise 15: Fifteen beats for every four bars

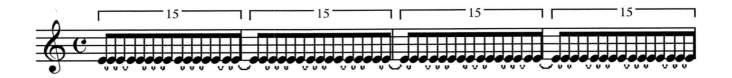

Exercise 16: Sixteen beats for every four bars

Rhythm Technique Two

Rhythm Technique Two will take you through 15 exercises which divide a four bar period of time into unequal subdivisions. It is not necessary to master all these 15 exercises before proceeding to the next technique. Each track on the CD will make these exercises easier or harder depending on the tempo. Experiment to find which track is a good starting place for you. You can approach these exercises in two ways: play all the quarter notes and accent the appropriate notes or play only the accented notes. You can also apply this unequal subdivision to all the exercises presented in Rhythm Technique One. This more advanced method will greatly strengthen your ability to subdivide 4 measures. But remember, always try to hear the rhythm rather than count it in your head. The following exercises are excerpts from "Accents Volume One" ISBN #1890944386

Exercise 1: A group of 3 and 5 within four bars

Exercise 2: A group of 5 and 3 within four bars

Exercise 3: A group of 1, 3 and 4 within four bars

Exercise 4: Three groups of 1, 4 and 3 within four bars

Exercise 5: Three groups divided 3-1-4 within four bars

Exercise 6: Three groups divided 3-4-1 within four bars

Exercise 7: Three groups divided 4-1-3 within four bars

Exercise 8: Three groups divided 4-3-1 within four bars

Exercise 9: Three groups divided 1-2-5 within four bars

Exercise 10: Three groups divided 1-5-2 within four bars

Exercise 11: Three groups divided 2-1-5 within four bars

Exercise 12: Three groups divided 2-5-1 within four bars

Exercise 13: Three groups divided 5-1-2 within four bars

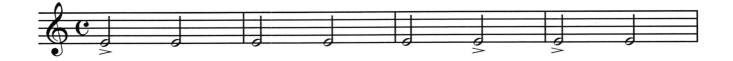

Exercise 14: Three groups divided 5-2-1 within four bars

Exercise 15: Three groups divided 2-5-1 within four bars

Part two of Technique Two looks at unequal subdivisions using quarter notes as the basic division of time. Unequal subdivisions could of course be applied to many metric levels. Experiment with eighth notes and other rhythms and you will find may interesting ways to apply accents.

Exercise 1: A group of 7 and 9 within four bars

Exercise 2: A group of 9 and 7 within four bars

Exercise 3: A group of 5 and 11 within four bars

Exercise 4: A group of 11 and 5 within four bars

Exercise 5: Three groups divided 5-4-7 within four bars

Exercise 6: Three groups divided 7-4-5 within four bars

Exercise 7: Three groups divided 7-6-3 within four bars

Exercise 8: Four groups divided 3-3-5-5 within four bars

Exercise 9: Four groups divided 3-3-5-5 within four bars

Exercise 10: Four groups divided 5-5-3-3 within four bars

Rhythm Technique Three

Rhythm Technique Three will take you through 8 exercises which present various rhythm patterns in a four bar period of time. The first 4 contain quarter note rhythms. The second 4 contain eighth note rhythms. It is not necessary to master all these 8 exercises before proceeding to the next technique. Each track on the CD will make these exercises easier or harder depending on the tempo. Experiment to find which track is a good starting place for you. The eighth note exercises are excerpts from "Rhythms Volume One" ISBN #0964863278

Exercise 1

Exercise 2

Exercise 3

Exercise 4

Exercise 5

Exercise 6

Exercise 7

Exercise 8

Rhythm Technique Four

Rhythm Technique Four will take you through 4 sixteenth note exercises which present various rhythm patterns in a four bar period of time. It is not necessary to master all these 4 exercises before proceeding to the next technique. Each track on the CD will make these exercises easier or harder depending on the tempo. Experiment to find which track is a good starting place for you. The following exercises are excerpts from "Rhythms Volume Two" ISBN #0964863286

Exercise 1

Exercise 2

Exercise 3

Exercise 4

Rhythm Technique Five

Rhythm Technique Five will take you through 4 exercises which present various odd meter combinations within a four bar period of time. First work on feeling the overall rhythm by playing only on 'one' of each measure. Then attempt the written rhythm. It is not necessary to master all these 4 exercises before proceeding to the next technique. Each track on the CD will make these exercises easier or harder depending on the tempo. Experiment to find which track is a good starting place for you. The following exercises are excerpts from "Odd Meters" ISBN #0964863294

Exercise 1

Exercise 2

Exercise 3

Exercise 4

Rhythm Technique Six

Rhythm Technique Six will take you through 13 exercises which promote a strong sense of time through development of independence within a four measure grouping. Play each part using a different limb. Work through all combinations to get the most out of this technique. The following is a list of possible combinations:

Right Hand   Left Hand
Right Hand   Right Foot
Right Hand   Left Foot
Left Hand   Right Hand
Left Hand   Left Foot
Left Hand   Right Foot
Right Foot   Left Foot
Right Foot   Right Hand
Right Foot   Left Hand
Left Foot   Right Foot
Left Foot   Left Hand
Left Foot   Right Hand

It is not necessary to master all these 13 exercises before proceeding to the next technique. Each track on the CD will make these exercises easier or harder depending on the tempo. Experiment to find which tempo is a good starting place for you. The following are excerpts from Independence Volume One ISBN # 1890944009.

Exercise 1:

Exercise 2

Exercise 3

Exercise 4

Exercise 5

Exercise 6

Exercise 7

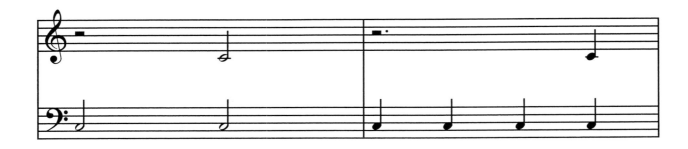

Exercise 8

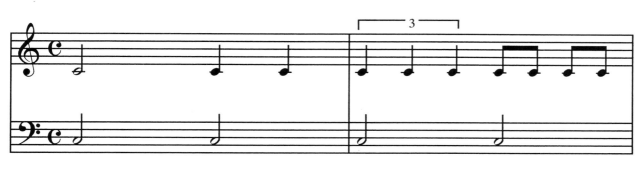

Exercise 9

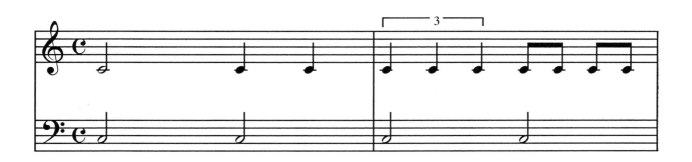

Exercise 10

Exercise 11

Exercise 12

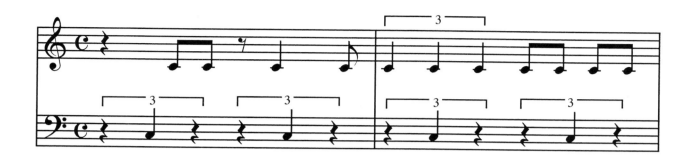

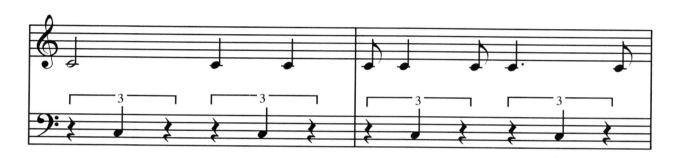

Exercise 13

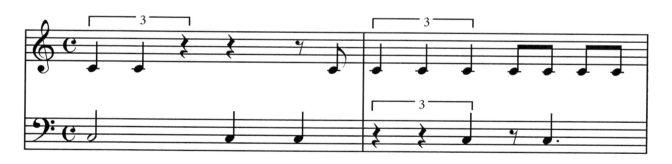

Melodic Techniques

Melodic Techniques to develop control within a four measure grouping can be approached many ways. The following exercises will show some of the ways you can develop a longer rhythmic sense and how this longer rhythmic sense can affect your melodic choices. You will find that thinking in a longer basic rhythm can have profound impact on your phrasing, rhythmic choices and melodic direction. The following exercises explore some of those choices.

Melodic Technique One

Melodic Technique One shows 2 exercises which show some of the possible ways a four measure grouping can effect the rhythmic placement of a melodic line. Example 1 and 2 present an example of a scale that can be used to create a melodic pattern that will repeat every four bars. Example 1 is a simple pentatonic scale grouped in a 8 note pattern which when played in eighth notes will repeat itself every four bars. Example 2 shows a major scale which when sequenced in eighth notes in a 24 note pattern will repeat itself every four bars. Pick various scales and melodic patterns that repeat every four bars and you can reinforce your feeling of a four bar phrase. Experiment with the rhythmic patterns found in the Rhythm Technique One section and you will find many new ways of playing melodically over four bars.

Exercise 1 is an example of playing a pentatonic scale in a regular phrasing pattern.

Exercise 2 is an example of playing a major scale in a regular phrasing pattern.

Melodic Technique Two

Melodic Technique Two will take you through 7 exercises which show how an irregular phrasing pattern can help to create variation within a melodic pattern. Example 1 shows a 10 note pattern in constant triplets. This creates an irregular pattern that only repeats itself every 20 bars. You will notice by looking at the markers every four bars that you start on a different beat every four measures. By practicing with this type of melodic pattern you become aware of how your phrasing changes, as opposed to using a metronome, where you don't have the feeling of a larger 4 measure group, but only a constant click that doesn't define the downbeat of a measure. Pick various scales and melodic patterns that repeat every four bars and you can reinforce your feeling for a four bar phrase. Experiment with the rhythmic patterns found in Rhythm Technique One and you will find many new ways of playing melodically over four bars.

Exercise 1

Exercise 2 presents a 6 note arpeggio which has irregular phrasing. This melodic pattern repeats itself every 10 notes but it takes 20 measures before the pattern is back to starting on 'one'.

Exercise 2

Exercise 3 presents a 3 note scale which has irregular phrasing. This melodic pattern repeats itself every 6 notes but it takes 12 measures before the pattern is back to starting on 'one'.

Exercise 3

Exercise 4 presents a 4 note scale which has irregular phrasing. This me-lodic pattern repeats itself every 8 notes but it takes 8 measures before the pattern is back to starting on 'one'.

Exercise 4

Exercise 5 presents a 6 note scale which has irregular phrasing. This melodic pattern repeats itself every 10 notes but it takes 20 measures before the pattern is back to starting on 'one'.

Exercise 5

Exercise 6 presents a 2 note scale which has irregular phrasing. This melodic pattern repeats itself every 8 notes but it takes 8 measures before the pattern is back to starting on 'one'.

Exercise 6

Melodic Technique Three

Melodic Technique Three involves playing Blues melodies, or "heads," to improve your ability to play an entire 12 bar melody with just one click every four bars. You could use any head found in a fake book. Some common examples of Jazz 12 bar blues are:

Au Privave
Blue Monk
Blues for Alice
Blue Train

On the next page I have given you a rather challenging head to a 12 Bar Blues entitled "A Few Dozen". Try playing this with various tracks on the CD. If you would like to hear a recording of this check out The Bruce Arnold Trio, "A Few Dozen" release date 1/1/2000.

A Few Dozen

Composer Bruce Arnold

A Few Dozen Bass Part

Composer Bruce Arnold

Harmonic Techniques

Harmonic Techniques to develop control within a four measure grouping can be approached many ways. I will mention a few here to get you started. One of the most exciting applications of this four bar period of time is to combine the previously discussed rhythm techniques with chord progressions. Also you can try some of the more obvious applications of the four bar grouping over 12 bar blues forms.

Harmonic Technique One

Harmonic Technique One presents 3 exercises where a harmonic framework is superimposed over some of the 4 measure rhythmic groupings presented on pages 3-6. It is beyond the scope of this book to explain the theories behind these chord progressions. A partial explanation of some of these techniques can be found in Chord Workbook for Guitar Volume One and Two
ISBN # 0964863219 and 0964863235.

Exercise 1: Use over 1st four bars of 12 Bar Blues in Gb

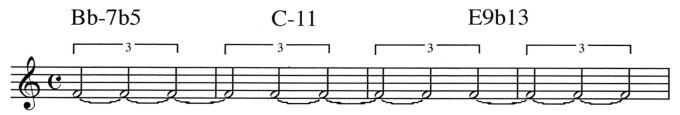

Exercise 2: Use over bars 3 and 4 of a 12 Bar Blues in Gb

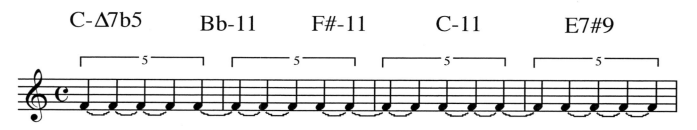

Exercise 3: Use over last four bars of a 12 Bar Blues in Gb

Harmonic Technique Two

Harmonic Technique Two presents two 12 bar chord progressions that can be used to develop an ability to play chords through a blues progression. If you play a melodic instrument try playing the chords as arpeggios. If you would like more 12 bar blues progressions I recommend Chord Workbook for Guitar Volume One ISBN # 0964863219 which contains 24 twelve bar blues progressions.

12 Bar Blues in Gb

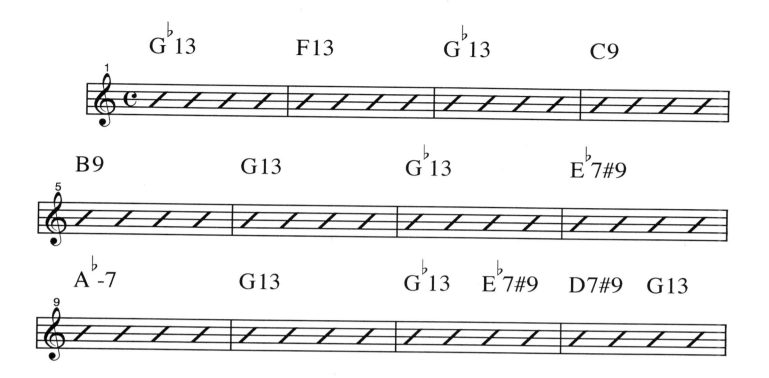

12 Bar Blues in B

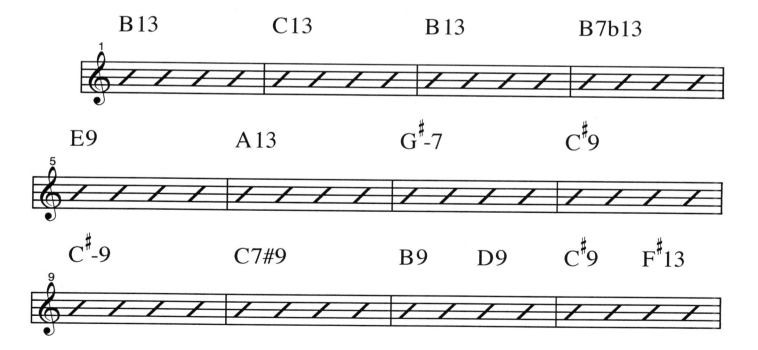

Creative Technique

I have written repeatedly about the creative approach, yet there is very little that one can do to teach this particular aspect of music. This is something that comes from within, and the best that any teacher can do is to provide every possible tool for the student so that there is no impediment to the creative process. Presenting more techniques of improvisation just brings us back to a technical side of music. It is best that you use this section of the book as a springboard for your self expression.

I have included some solo forms using the traditional major and minor blues. As with all solo forms there are infinite variations you can use to practice and be creative. Much of your direction in this section depends on your instrument. If you are a drummer or a piano player your can just play time or play the chords. If you are a saxophonist you may express yourself in a multitude of ways, from free form blowing to structured scales. It all depends on where you are with music and where you are going. This is why for this section of the book I have just supplied some chord progressions that you can use to improvise with. Experiment and try different approaches to test your ability to keep time flowing correctly. From the work you have done in the technical section of this book you should find that you are able to function more efficiently within a 4 bar phrase. The real challenge comes when you let go and completely trust your internal clock as you improvise. This is the key to letting your inner voice speak. It is a lifelong pursuit for the artist that is within you.

12 Bar Blues in E

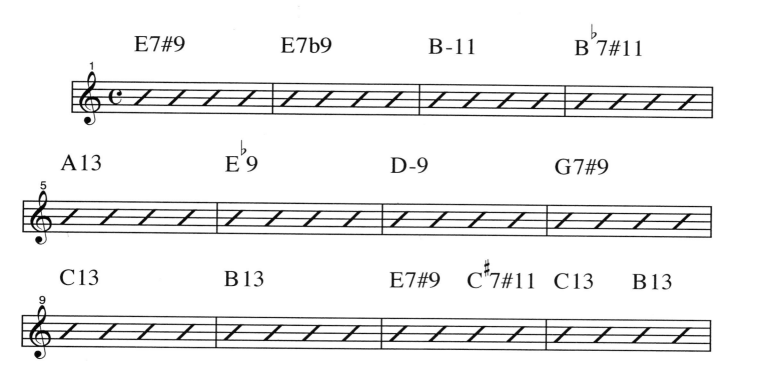

12 Bar Blues in A

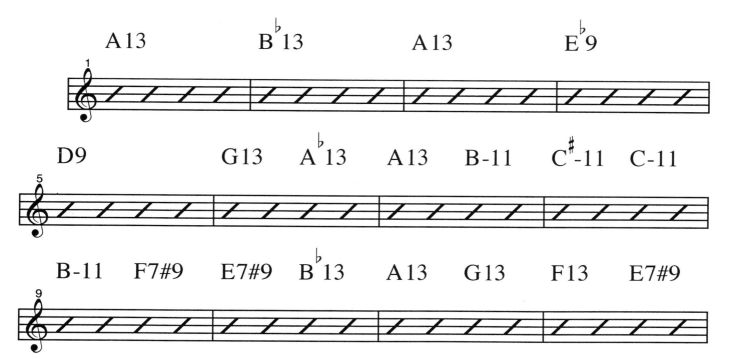

12 Bar Blues in D

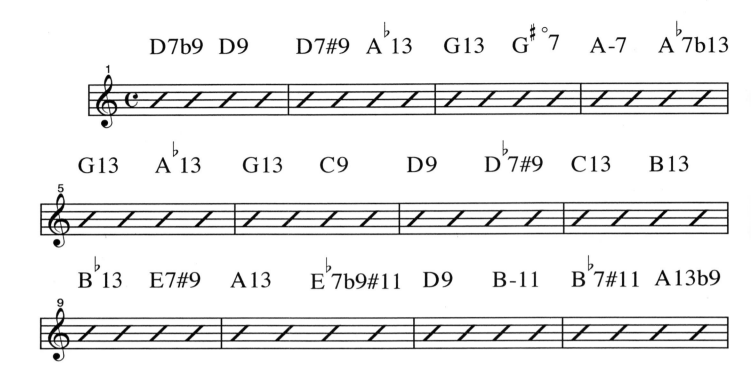

12 Bar Blues in G

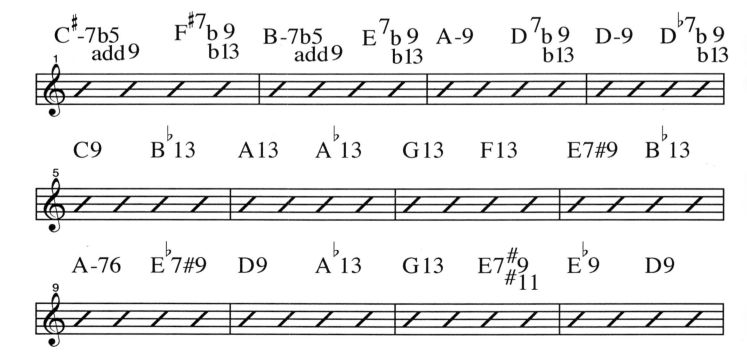

Gb Minor Blues

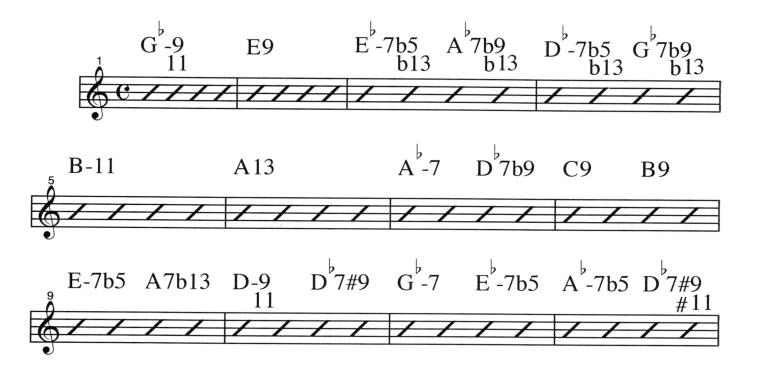

B Minor Blues

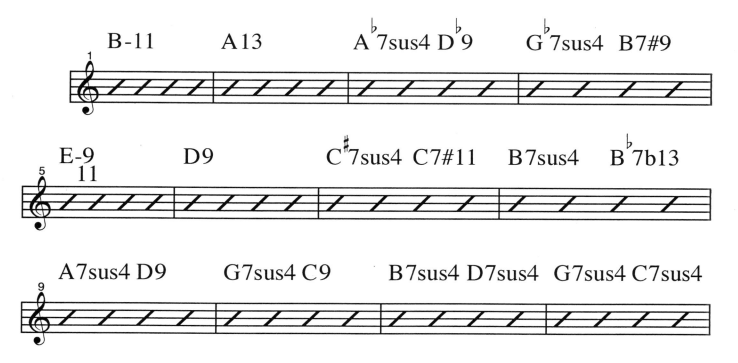

E Minor Blues

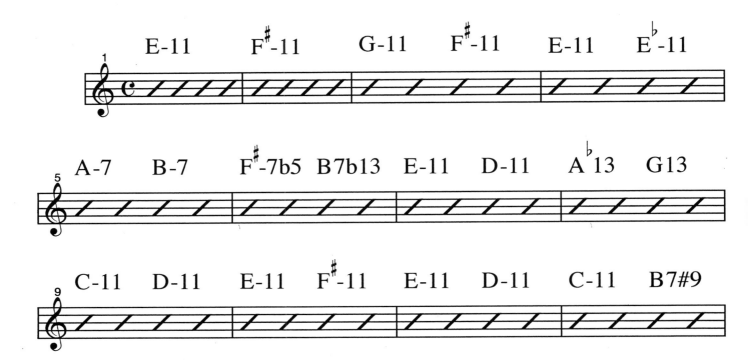

A Minor Blues

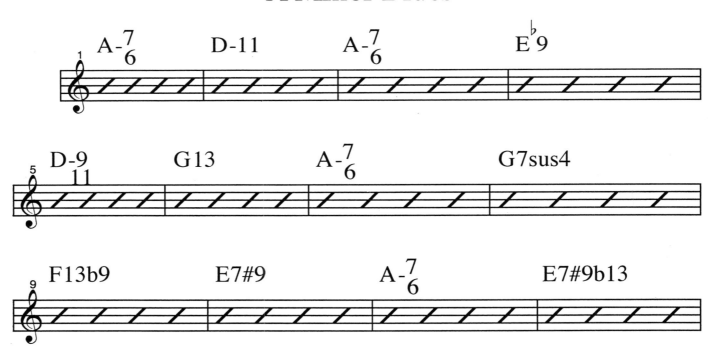

Books Available From
Muse Eek Publishing Company

The Bruce Arnold series of instruction books for guitar are the result of 20 years of teaching. Mr. Arnold, who teaches at New York University and Princeton University has listened to the questions and problems of his students, and written forty books addressing the needs of the beginning to advanced student. Written in a direct, friendly and practical manner, each book is structured in such as way as to enable a student to understand, retain and apply musical information. In short, these books teach.

Chord Workbook for Guitar Volume 1 (2nd edition)
ISBN 0-9648632-1-9

A consistent seller, this book addresses the needs of the beginning through intermediate student. The beginning student will learn chords on the guitar, and a section is also included to help learn the basics of music theory. Progressions are provided to help a student apply these chords to common sequences. The more advanced student will find the reharmonization section to be an invaluable resource of harmonic choices. Information is given through musical notation as well as tablature.

Chord Workbook for Guitar Volume 2 (2nd edition)
ISBN 0-9648632-3-5

This book is the Rosetta stone of pop/jazz chords, and is geared to the intermediate to advanced student. *These are the chords that any serious student bent on a musical career must know.* Unlike other books which simply give examples of isolated chords, this unique book provides a comprehensive series of progressions and chord combinations which are immediately applicable to both composition and performance.

Music Theory Workbook for Guitar Series

The world's most popular instrument, the guitar, is not taught in our public schools. In addition, it is one of the hardest on which to learn the basics of music. As a result, it is frequently difficult for the serious guitarist to get a firm foundation in theory.

Theory Workbook for Guitar Volume 1 ISBN 0-9648632-4-3

This book provides real hands-on application of intervals and chords. A theory section written in concise and easy to understand language prepares the student for all exercises. Worksheets are given that quiz a student about intervals and chord construction using staff notation and guitar tablature. Answers are supplied in the back of the book enabling a student to work without a teacher.

To order books:
from your local music store, bookstore use the ISBN number or
on-line at amazon.com and barnesandnoble.com
or direct from:

Muse Eek Publishing Company
550 Broadway 2nd Floor
New York, New York 10012
phone: 212-226-9479   fax: 212-625-1839

Audio examples and more information can be found on the internet at www.muse-eek.com

Theory Workbook for Guitar Volume 2 ISBN   0-9648632-5-1

This book provides real hands-on application for 22 different scale types.   A theory section written in concise and easy to understand language prepares the student for all exercises.   Worksheets are given that quiz a student about scale construction using staff notation and guitar tablature.   Answers are supplied in the back of the book enabling a student to work without a teacher.   Audio files are also available on the muse-eek.com website to facilitate practice and improvisation with all the scales presented.

Rhythm Book Series

These books are a breakthrough in music instruction, using the internet as a teaching tool! Audio files of all the exercises are easily downloaded from the internet.

Rhythm Primer ISBN   0-890944-03-3

This 61 page book concentrates on all basic rhythms using four rhythmic levels.   All examples use one pitch, allowing the student to focus completely on time and rhythm.   All exercises can be downloaded from the internet to facilitate learning.   See http://www.muse-eek.com for details.

Rhythms Volume 1 ISBN   0-9648632-7-8

This 120 page book concentrates on eighth note rhythms and is a thesaurus of rhythmic patterns.   All examples use one pitch, allowing the student to focus completely on time and rhythm.   All exercises can be downloaded from the internet to facilitate learning. See http://www.muse-eek.com for details.

Rhythms Volume 2 ISBN   0-9648632-8-6

This volume concentrates on sixteenth note rhythms, and is a 108 page thesaurus of rhythmic patterns.   All examples use one pitch, allowing the student to focus completely on time and rhythm.   All exercises can be downloaded from the internet to facilitate learning. See http://www.muse-eek.com for details.

Rhythms Volume 3 ISBN   0-890944-04-1

This volume concentrates on thirty second note rhythms, and is a 102 page thesaurus of rhythmic patterns.   All examples use one pitch, allowing the student to focus completely on time and rhythm.   All exercises can be downloaded from the internet to facilitate learning. See http://www.muse-eek.com for details.

To order books:
from your local music store, bookstore use the ISBN number or
on-line at amazon.com and barnesandnoble.com
or direct from:

Muse Eek Publishing Company
550 Broadway 2nd Floor
New York, New York 10012
phone: 212-226-9479   fax: 212-625-1839

Audio examples and more information can be found on the internet at www.muse-eek.com

Odd Meters Volume 1 ISBN 0-9648632-9-4

This book applies both eighth and sixteenth note rhythms to odd meter combinations. All examples use one pitch, allowing the student to focus completely on time and rhythm. Exercises can be downloaded from the internet to facilitate learning. This 100 page book is an essential sight reading tool.
See http://www.muse-eek.com for details.

Contemporary Rhythms Volume 1 ISBN 1-890944-27-0

This volume concentrates on eight note rhythms and is a thesaurus of rhythmic patterns. Each exercise uses one pitch which allows the student to focus completely on time and rhythm. Exercises use modern innovations common to twentieth century notation, thereby familiarizing the student with the most sophisticated systems likely to be encountered in the course of a musical career. All exercises can be downloaded from the internet to facilitate learning. See http://www.muse-eek.com for details.

Contemporary Rhythms Volume 2 ISBN 1-890944-28-9

This volume concentrates on sixteenth note rhythms and is a thesaurus of rhythmic patterns. Each exercise uses one pitch which allows the student to focus completely on time and rhythm. Exercise use modern innovations common to twentieth century notation, thereby familiarizing the student with the most sophisticated systems likely to be encountered in the course of a musical career. All exercises can be downloaded from the internet to facilitate learning. See http://www.muse-eek.com for details.

Independence Volume 1   ISBN 1-890944-00-9

This 51 page book is designed for pianists, stick and touchstyle guitarists, percussionists and anyone who wishes to develop the rhythmic independence of their hands. This volume concentrates on quarter, eighth and sixteenth note rhythms and is a thesaurus of rhythmic patterns. The exercises in this book gradually incorporate more and more complex rhythmic patterns making it an excellent tool for both the beginning and the advanced student.

Other Guitar Study Aids

Right Hand Technique for Guitar Volume 1
ISBN 0-9648632-6-X

Here's a breakthrough in music instruction, using the internet as a teaching tool! This book gives a concise method for developing right hand technique on the guitar, one of the most overlooked and under-addressed aspects of learning the instrument. The simplest, most basic movements are used to build fatigue-free and virtuousic technique. Exercises can be downloaded from the internet to facilitate learning. See http://www.muse-eek.com for details.

To order books:
from your local music store, bookstore use the ISBN number or
on-line at amazon.com and barnesandnoble.com
or direct from:

Muse Eek Publishing Company
550 Broadway 2nd Floor
New York, New York 10012
phone: 212-226-9479   fax: 212-625-1839

Audio examples and more information can be found on the internet at www.muse-eek.com

Single String Studies Volume One ISBN 1-890944-01-7

This book is an excellent learning tool for both the beginner who has no experience reading music on the guitar, and the advanced student looking to improve their ledger line reading and general knowledge of each string of the guitar. Each exercise concentrates a students attention of one string at a time. This allows a familiarity to form between the written pitch and where it can be found on the guitar along with improving one's "feel" for jumping linearly across the guitar neck. Exercises can be downloaded from the internet to facilitate learning. See http://www.muse-eek.com for details.

Single String Studies Volume Two ISBN 1-890944-05-X

This book is a continuation of volume one but now using non-diatonic notes. Volume two helps the intermediate and advanced student improve their ledger line reading and general knowledge of each string of the guitar. Each exercise concentrates a students attention of one string at a time. This allows a familiarity to form between the written pitch and where it can be found on the guitar along with improving one's "feel" for jumping linearly across the guitar neck. Exercises can be downloaded from the internet to facilitate learning. See http://www.muse-eek.com for details.

Single String Studies Volume One (Bass Clef) ISBN 1-890944-02-5

This book is an excellent learning tool for both the beginner who has no experience reading music on the bass guitar, and the advanced student looking to improve their ledger line reading and general knowledge of each string of the bass. Each exercise concentrates a students attention of one string at a time. This allows a familiarity to form between the written pitch and where it can be found on the bass along with improving one's "feel" for jumping linearly across the fretboard. Exercises can be downloaded from the internet to facilitate learning. See http://www.muse-eek.com for details.

Single String Studies Volume Two (Bass Clef) ISBN 1-890944-06-8

This book is a continuation of volume one but now using non-diatonic notes. Volume two helps the intermediate and advanced student improve their ledger line reading and general knowledge of each string of the bass. Each exercise concentrates a students attention of one string at a time. This allows a familiarity to form between the written pitch and where it can be found on the bass along with improving one's "feel" for jumping linearly across the fretboard. Exercises can be downloaded from the internet to facilitate learning. See http://www.muse-eek.com for details.

To order books:
from your local music store, bookstore use the ISBN number or
on-line at amazon.com and barnesandnoble.com
or direct from:

Muse Eek Publishing Company
550 Broadway 2nd Floor
New York, New York 10012
phone: 212-226-9479   fax: 212-625-1839

Audio examples and more information can be found on the internet at www.muse-eek.com

Sight Singing and Ear Training Series

The world is full of ear training and sight reading books, so why do we need more? This sight singing and ear training series uses a different method of teaching relative pitch sight singing and ear training. The success of this method has been astounding. Along with a new method of ear training these books also use CDs and the internet as a teaching tool! Audio files of all the exercises are easily downloaded from the internet at www.muse-eek.com By combining interactive audio files with a new approach to ear training a student's progress is limited only by their willingness to practice!

A Fanatic's Guide to Ear Training and Sight Singing
ISBN 1-890944-19-X

This book and CD present a method for developing good pitch recognition through sight singing. This method differs from the myriad of other sight singing books in that it develops the ability to identify and name all twelve pitches within a key center. Through this method a student gains the ability to identify sound based on it's relationship to a key and not the relationship of one note to another i.e. interval training as commonly taught in many texts. All note groupings from one to six notes are presented giving the student a thesaurus of basic note combinations which develops sight singing and note recognition to a level unattainable before this Guide's existence.

Key Center Recognition ISBN 1-890944-30-3

This book and CD present a method for developing the ability to recognize the function of any note against a key. This method is a must for anyone who wishes to sound one note on an instrument or voice and instantly know what key a song is in. Through this method a student gains the ability to identify a sound based on its relationship to a key and not the relationship of one note to another i.e. interval training as commonly taught in many texts. Key Center Recognition is a definite requirement before proceeding to two note ear training.

LINES Volume One: Sight Reading and Sight Singing Exercises
ISBN 1-890944-09-2

This book can be used for many applications. It is an excellent source for easy half note melodies that a beginner can use to learn how to read music or for sight singing slightly chromatic lines. An intermediate or advanced student will find exercises for multi-voice reading. These exercises can also be used for multi-voice ear training. The book has the added benefit in that all exercises can be heard by downloading the audio files for each example. See http://www.muse-eek.com for details.

Ear Training ONE NOTE: Beginning Level   ISBN 1-890944-12-2

This Book and Audio CD presents a new and exciting method of developing relative pitch ear training. It has been used with great success and is now finally available on CD. There are three levels available depending on the student's ability. There are three levels available depending on

To order books:
from your local music store, bookstore use the ISBN number or
on-line at amazon.com and barnesandnoble.com
or direct from:

Muse Eek Publishing Company
550 Broadway 2nd Floor
New York, New York 10012
phone: 212-226-9479   fax: 212-625-1839

Audio examples and more information can be found on the internet at www.muse-eek.com

the student's ability. This beginning level is recommended for students who have little or no music training.

Ear Training ONE NOTE: Intermediate Level   ISBN 1-890944-13-0

This Audio CD and booklet presents a new and exciting method of developing relative pitch ear training. It has been used with great success and is now finally available on CD. This intermediate level is recommended for students who have had some music training but still find their skills need more development.

Ear Training ONE NOTE: Advanced Level   ISBN 1-890944-14-9

This Audio CD and booklet presents a new and exciting method of developing relative pitch ear training. It has been used with great success and is now finally available on CD. There are three levels available depending on the student's ability. This advanced level is recommended for students who have worked with the intermediate level and now wish to perfect their skills.

Ear Training TWO NOTE: Beginning Level Volume One
ISBN 1-890944-31-9

This Book and Audio CD continues the new and exciting method of developing relative pitch ear training as set forth in the "Ear Training, One Note" series. There are six volume in the beginning level series. Through practice, the student eventually gains the ability to recognize the key and the names of any two notes played simultaneously. Volume One concentrates on 5ths. Prerequisite: a strong grasp of the One Note method.

Ear Training TWO NOTE: Beginning Level Volume Two
ISBN 1-890944-32-7

This Book and Audio CD continues the new and exciting method of developing relative pitch ear training as set forth in the "Ear Training, One Note" series. There are six volume in the beginning level series. Through practice, the student eventually gains the ability to recognize the key and the names of any two notes played simultaneously. Volume Two concentrates on 3rds. Prerequisite: a strong grasp of the One Note method.

Ear Training TWO NOTE: Beginning Level Volume Three
ISBN 1-890944-33-5

This Book and Audio CD continues the new and exciting method of developing relative pitch ear training as set forth in the "Ear Training, One Note" series. There are six volume in the beginning level series. Through practice, the student eventually gains the ability to recognize the key and the names of any two notes played simultaneously. Volume Three concentrates on 6ths. Prerequisite: a strong grasp of the One Note method.

To order books:
from your local music store, bookstore use the ISBN number or
on-line at amazon.com and barnesandnoble.com
or direct from:

Muse Eek Publishing Company
550 Broadway 2nd Floor
New York, New York 10012
phone: 212-226-9479   fax: 212-625-1839

Audio examples and more information can be found on the internet at www.muse-eek.com

Ear Training TWO NOTE: Beginning Level Volume Four
ISBN 1-890944-34-3

This Book and Audio CD continues the new and exciting method of developing relative pitch ear training as set forth in the "Ear Training, One Note" series. There are six volume in the beginning level series. Through practice, the student eventually gains the ability to recognize the key and the names of any two notes played simultaneously. Volume Four concentrates on 4ths. Prerequisite: a strong grasp of the One Note method.

Ear Training TWO NOTE: Beginning Level Volume Five
ISBN 1-890944-35-1

This Book and Audio CD continues the new and exciting method of developing relative pitch ear training as set forth in the "Ear Training, One Note" series. There are six volume in the beginning level series. Through practice, the student eventually gains the ability to recognize the key and the names of any two notes played simultaneously. Volume Five concentrates on 2nds. Prerequisite: a strong grasp of the One Note method.

Ear Training TWO NOTE: Beginning Level Volume Six
ISBN 1-890944-36-X

This Book and Audio CD continues the new and exciting method of developing relative pitch ear training as set forth in the "Ear Training, One Note" series. There are six volume in the beginning level series. Through practice, the student eventually gains the ability to recognize the key and the names of any two notes played simultaneously. Volume Six concentrates on 7ths. Prerequisite: a strong grasp of the One Note method.

Comping Styles Series

This series builds off from the progressions found in Chord Workbook Volume One. Each book covers a specific style of music and presents exercises to help a guitarist, bassist or drummer master that style. Audio CDs are also available so a student can play along with each example and really get "into the groove".

Comping Styles for the Guitar Volume Two FUNK
ISBN 1-890944-07-6

This volume teaches a student how to play guitar or piano in a funk style. 36 Progressions are presented: 12 keys of a Major and Minor Blues plus 12 keys of Rhythm Changes A different groove is presented for each exercise giving the student a wide range of funk rhythms to master. An Audio CD is also included so a student can play along with each example and really get "into the groove". The audio CD contains "trio" versions of each exercise with Guitar, Bass and Drums.

To order books:
from your local music store, bookstore use the ISBN number or
on-line at amazon.com and barnesandnoble.com
or direct from:

Muse Eek Publishing Company
550 Broadway 2nd Floor
New York, New York 10012
phone: 212-226-9479   fax: 212-625-1839

Audio examples and more information can be found on the internet at www.muse-eek.com

Comping Styles for the Bass Volume Two FUNK
ISBN 1-890944-08-4

This volume teaches a student how to play bass in a funk style. 36 Progressions are presented: 12 keys of a Major and Minor Blues plus 12 keys of Rhythm Changes A different groove is presented for each exercise giving the student a wide range of funk rhythms to master. An Audio CD is also included so a student can play along with each example and really get "into the groove". The audio CD contains "trio" versions of each exercise with Guitar, Bass and Drums.

Time   Series

The Doing Time series presents a method for gaining control of your internal time sense: This series is an excellent source for any musician who is serious about developing strong internal sense of time. This is particularly useful in any kind of music where the rhythms and time signatures may be very complex or free, and there is no conductor.

THE BIG METRONOME
ISBN   1-890944-37-8

The Big Metronome is designed to help you develop a better internal sense of time. This is accomplished by requiring you to "feel time" rather than having you rely on the steady click of a metronome. The idea is to slowly wean yourself away from an external device and rely on your internal/natural sense of time. The exercises presented work in conjunction with the three CDs that accompany this book. CD 1 presents the first 13 settings from a traditional metronome 40-66; the second CD contains metronome markings 69-116, and the third CD contains metronome markings 120-208. The first CD gives you a 2 bar count off and a click every measure, the second CD gives you a 2 bar count off and a click every 2 measures, the 3rd CD gives you a 2 bar count off and a click every 4 measures. By presenting all common metronome markings a student can use these 3 CDs as a replacement for a traditional metronome.

Doing Time with the Blues Volume One:
ISBN 1-890944-17-3

The book and CD presents a method for gaining an internal sense of time thereby eliminating dependence on a metronome.. The book presents the basic concept for developing good time and also includes exercises that can be practiced with the CD. The CD provides eight 8 minute tracks at different tempos in which the time is delineated every 2 bars, and with an extra hit every 12 bars to outline the blues form. The student may then use the exercises presented in the book to gain control of their execution or improvise to gain control of their ideas using this bare minimum of time delineation.

To order books:
from your local music store, bookstore use the ISBN number or
on-line at amazon.com and barnesandnoble.com
or direct from:

Muse Eek Publishing Company
550 Broadway 2nd Floor
New York, New York 10012
phone: 212-226-9479   fax: 212-625-1839

Audio examples and more information can be found on the internet at www.muse-eek.com